TEAM SPIRIT®

SMART BOOKS FOR YOUNG FANS

THE MINNESOTA TWINS

BY

MARK STEWART

New Hanover County Public Library
201 Chestnut Street
Wilmington, North Carolina 28401

NORWOOD HOUSE PRESS
CHICAGO, ILLINOIS

Norwood House Press
P.O. Box 316598
Chicago, Illinois 60631

For information regarding Norwood House Press, please visit our website at:
www.norwoodhousepress.com or call 866-565-2900.

All photos courtesy of Getty Images except the following:
SportsChrome (4, 10, 11, 12, 14, 36, 39), Author's Collection (6, 15, 33), Tom DiPace (8),
Black Book Partners Archives (9, 17, 35 all, 43 bottom left, 45), Exhibit Supply Co. (16),
Topps, Inc. (21, 29, 31, 34 top and bottom right, 37, 42 bottom, 43 top & bottom right),
Bowman Gum Co. (24), Gum Inc. (28), Sweet Caporal (34 bottom left),
General Mills (38), Fleer Corp. (41), Ziv Television Productions (42 top), Matt Richman (48).
Cover Photo: Hannah Foslien/Getty Images

The memorabilia and artifacts pictured in this book are presented for educational and informational purposes,
and come from the collection of the author.

Editor: Mike Kennedy
Designer: Ron Jaffe
Project Management: Black Book Partners, LLC.
Special thanks to Topps, Inc.

Library of Congress Cataloging-in-Publication Data

Stewart, Mark, 1960-
  The Minnesota Twins / by Mark Stewart. -- Library ed.
    p. cm. -- (Team spirit)
  Includes bibliographical references and index.
  Summary: "A Team Spirit Baseball edition featuring the Minnesota Twins
that chronicles the history and accomplishments of the team. Includes access
to the Team Spirit website, which provides additional information, updates
and photos"--Provided by publisher.
  ISBN 978-1-59953-488-6 (library : alk. paper) -- ISBN 978-1-60357-368-9
(ebook) 1. Minnesota Twins (Baseball team)--History--Juvenile literature.
I. Title.
  GV875.M55S74 2012
  796.357'6409776579--dc23
                                        2011048467

Manufactured in the United States of America in North Mankato, Minnesota.
196N—012012

COVER PHOTO: The Twins and their fans celebrate a home run during a 2011 game.

TABLE OF CONTENTS

ABOUT OUR GLOSSARY

In this book, there may be several words that you are reading for the first time. Some are sports words, some are new vocabulary words, and some are familiar words that are used in an unusual way. All of these words are defined on page 46. Throughout the book, sports words appear in **bold type**. Regular vocabulary words appear in ***bold italic type***.

MEET THE TWINS

If a player swings the bat well, he can always find a home with the Minnesota Twins. That has been true for more than 50 years. Indeed, the Twins have a *tradition* of home run hitters and batting champions that few teams can match.

Of course, there is much more to Minnesota's success than power at the plate. The Twins pride themselves on playing good, smart baseball. They are prepared for every situation. The Twins know how to win games on the basepaths and in the field. And their pitchers are always thinking a step ahead of enemy batters.

This book tells the story of the Twins. They are known for their big hitters, but they also have a knack for doing all the little things that lead to victory. When they are at the top of their game, there is no team in baseball that's harder to beat.

The Twins escort hometown hero Joe Mauer to the dugout after he scores a run. Mauer grew up in Minnesota watching the team play.

GLORY DAYS

The Twins played their first season in Minnesota in 1961. However, they were not a new team. Six *decades* earlier, the Washington Senators were one of eight teams that joined the newly formed **American League (AL)**. The team's greatest star in those early years was Walter Johnson, a sidearm pitcher who threw the ball close to 100 miles per hour. Another important person in the club's history was Clark Griffith. He began as the manager and ended up owning the team.

The Senators won the **World Series** in 1924. They captured the **pennant** twice after that, in 1925 and 1933. They had some very good players over the years, including Sam Rice, Goose Goslin, Joe Cronin, Heinie Manush, George Case, Cecil Travis, Sid Hudson, and Mickey Vernon. However, most seasons, the Senators finished at the bottom

of the standings. In fact, a popular joke said that Washington was "first in war, first in peace—and last in the American League."

By the 1950s, Griffith's nephew, Calvin, had taken charge of the team. The Senators were losing a lot of games—and a lot of money. Several baseball-starved cities offered to give the team a new home. In the end, the state of Minnesota won over the Griffith family. The team moved to the city of Bloomington in 1961 and played in brand-new Metropolitan Stadium. The Senators would forever after be known as the Twins.

Minnesota held onto some very good players from Washington. Jim Kaat and Camilo Pascual were among the best pitchers in the AL, while sluggers Harmon Killebrew and Bob Allison led the hitting attack.

By 1965, the Twins had a lineup that also included Zoilo Versalles, Tony Oliva, Jim Perry, and Mudcat Grant. That season, they won 102 games and reached the World Series.

The Twins were known as one of the hardest-hitting teams in baseball. In 1967, Killebrew and Oliva were joined by Rod Carew. He would win seven batting championships with the Twins. In the 1970s, top players such as Bert Blyleven, Bill Campbell, Butch Wynegar, and Roy Smalley also wore the Minnesota uniform. Despite these stars, the team went more than 20 seasons without winning another pennant. Many blamed Griffith, who was unwilling to pay his players high salaries.

Finally, in 1987, the Twins returned to the World Series. Led by Frank Viola, Kent Hrbek, Gary Gaetti, and Kirby Puckett, they became champions for the first time since moving to Minnesota. In 1991, the Twins won it all again. Puckett was the heart of those teams.

LEFT: Kirby Puckett   **ABOVE**: Kent Hrbek

He was a great hitter and fielder. His love of baseball rubbed off on everyone around him.

After their two championships, the Twins suffered through several losing seasons. In 2002, **Major League Baseball** considered eliminating the Twins or moving the team to a new city. For a brief moment, no one knew whether the Twins would survive!

The players responded like champions. Minnesota won 94 games and finished first in the **AL Central** in 2002. The Twins repeated as champions in 2003, 2004, 2006, 2009, and 2010. They were powered by Joe Mauer, the best hitting catcher anyone had ever seen. He teamed with first baseman Justin Morneau to give the Twins an exciting, high-scoring offense. Both players would go on to be named the league's **Most Valuable Player (MVP)**.

The Twins often find themselves competing against teams that can afford to offer big contracts to superstar players. Yet in most seasons, the Twins end up with one of the best records in baseball. The secret to Minnesota's success is that everyone on the club believes in each other—and in their ability to find a way to win. Whether young players come up from the **minor leagues** or join the Twins from other teams, they not only feel like family. They feel like winners.

LEFT: Joe Mauer led the league in hitting in 2006, 2008, and 2009.
ABOVE: Justin Morneau was the 2006 MVP.

HOME TURF

I n 1982, the Twins played their first season in the Hubert H. Humphrey Metrodome, which was named after Minnesota's beloved Senator. The stadium's *artificial* playing surface was notable because it was so springy. A short hit sometimes bounced right over the outfielder's head and rolled to the wall. The Metrodome was also very loud, especially when fans started screaming and waving their "Homer Hankies."

In 2010, the Twins moved into a new outdoor stadium. It is located near downtown Minneapolis. Fans sitting behind home plate can see beautiful views of the city skyline. Out behind the right field fence is a large gathering area for fans that includes statues of Kirby Puckett, Rod Carew, and Harmon Killebrew.

BY THE NUMBERS

- *The Twins' stadium has 39,504 seats.*
- *The distance from home plate to the left field foul pole is 339 feet.*
- *The distance from home plate to the center field fence is 411 feet.*
- *The distance from home plate to the right field foul pole is 328 feet.*

The Twins play a game in their new ballpark in 2010.

DRESSED FOR SUCCESS

The first uniforms worn by the Twins were almost identical to the ones from Washington in 1960. The team colors were white with scarlet and navy blue. The team name was written in slanted script across the front of the jersey. The home uniforms featured **pinstripes**, while the road uniforms were a bluish gray.

Minnesota's cap had an interlocking *T* and *C*, which stood for Twin Cities. A patch on the sleeve showed the team's new **logo**—twin baseball players from Minneapolis and St. Paul shaking hands across the Mississippi River.

During the 1970s and 1980s, the Twins switched to a modern-looking uniform. They went back to a more traditional style in 1987 and won their first championship. Today, the Twins usually wear a pinstripe uniform for home games that is very similar to the 1980s style. They also returned to the *TC* cap logo.

LEFT: Scott Baker fires a pitch in the Twins' 2011 road uniform.
ABOVE: Tony Oliva wears the team's uniform from the mid-1970s.

WE WON!

Some teams win championships by overwhelming their opponents. The Twins do things a little differently. They have won the World Series three times—twice in Minnesota and once as the Washington Senators. In every instance, they gave their fans incredible victories after standing at the very edge of defeat.

The Senators were the first "comeback kings." The year was 1924, and their World Series opponents were the New York Giants.

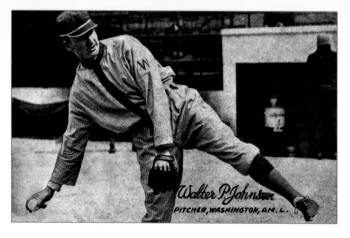

Washington was hoping that 36-year-old Walter Johnson would pitch them to victory. The Senators fell behind after five games. Pitcher Tom Zachary was great in a 2–1 victory in Game 6. That set up the dramatic Game 7.

The two teams battled through seven innings and the Giants held a 3–1 lead. The Senators loaded the bases with two out in the eighth, and **player-manager** Bucky Harris came to the plate. He hit a grounder to third, and it looked

LEFT: Walter Johnson warms up before a game.
RIGHT: Kirby Puckett greets Kent Hrbek after his grand slam in the 1987 World Series.

like Washington had wasted its last chance. But luck was on the Senators' side—the ball struck a pebble and bounced high over the fielder's head. Two runners scored and the game eventually went into extra innings tied 3–3. Harris called in Johnson to stop the Giants, and he held them scoreless inning after inning. In the 12th inning, Washington's Earl McNeely hit a double and Muddy Ruel crossed home plate with the championship-winning run.

Sixty-three years later, in 1987, the Twins once again found themselves trailing in the World Series, three games to two—this time to the St. Louis Cardinals. In Game 6, Kent Hrbek got the big hit for Minnesota. He blasted a **grand slam** to help the Twins win 11–5. In Game 7, with the crowd noise from Twins' fans almost deafening,

Frank Viola held the Cardinals to two runs with help from reliever Jeff Reardon. The Twins scratched out single runs in four different innings to win 4–2. Minnesota had its first championship.

The 1991 World Series was even more exciting. In fact, it was one of the best ever played. The Twins had added **All-Star** pitcher Jack Morris to their team, and he beat the Atlanta Braves in Game 1. The Twins won the next game on a dramatic eighth-inning home run, but the Braves did not quit. They won the next three and took a three games to two lead.

The Twins did not give up. In Game 6, Kirby Puckett hit a home run in the 11th inning to give Minnesota a 4–3 victory. Puckett had a hand in every Minnesota run and made one of the best catches in World Series history, too.

The next day, in Game 7, Morris and Atlanta's John Smoltz pitched one scoreless inning after another. As the

ABOVE: Tom Kelly led the Twins to a pair of championships.   **RIGHT**: Jack Morris pitches against the Atlanta Braves in 1991.

game wore on, it became clear that whichever team managed to cross home plate first would be the world champion. Once again, the game went into extra innings. Never before had the final World Series game gone so long without a run.

Manager Tom Kelly told Morris that he wanted to take him out, but the exhausted pitcher refused. Morris held the Braves in the top of the 10th inning, and then watched as teammate Dan Gladden hit a bloop double to start the bottom of the 10th. After Chuck Knoblauch bunted

Gladden to third, the Braves loaded the bases to create a force-out at any base. Kelly sent pinch-hitter Gene Larkin to the plate. With the fans on the edges of their seats, Larkin hit a single to give the Twins the championship.

GO-TO GUYS

To be a true star in baseball, you need more than a quick bat and a strong arm. You have to be a "go-to guy"—someone the manager wants on the pitcher's mound or in the batter's box when it matters most. Fans of the Senators and Twins have had a lot to cheer about over the years, including these great stars …

THE PIONEERS

WALTER JOHNSON   Pitcher

• BORN: 11/6/1887   • DIED: 12/10/1946   • PLAYED FOR TEAM: 1907 TO 1927
Walter Johnson threw his legendary fastball with a whipping motion that made it very difficult to see. He led the AL in strikeouts 12 times and was one of the first players voted into the Hall of Fame.

HARMON KILLEBREW   First Baseman/Third Baseman/Outfielder

• BORN: 6/29/1936   • DIED: 5/17/2011   • PLAYED FOR TEAM: 1954 TO 1974
Harmon Killebrew was the best player the Twins brought over from Washington when they moved in 1961. He was one of history's most feared sluggers. Killebrew was an All-Star 10 times from 1961 to 1971 and the AL MVP in 1969.

TONY OLIVA Outfielder

- BORN: 7/20/1938 • PLAYED FOR TEAM: 1962 TO 1976

Tony Oliva was an incredible hitter. He won the batting championship in his first two full seasons. He also led the league in this five times. Unfortunately, a knee injury cut his career short.

ROD CAREW Second Baseman/First Baseman

- BORN: 10/1/1945
- PLAYED FOR TEAM: 1967 TO 1978

Rod Carew was one of the smartest batters in history. He could hit any pitch hard and place the ball wherever he pleased. Carew won seven batting championships with the Twins, including six from 1972 to 1978.

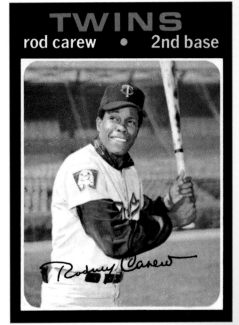

BERT BLYLEVEN Pitcher

- BORN: 4/6/1951
- PLAYED FOR TEAM: 1970 TO 1976 & 1985 TO 1988

Bert Blyleven joined the Twins as a teenager. He already had one of the best curveballs anyone had ever seen. In all, he won 149 games for Minnesota and struck out more than 2,000 batters. In 2011, Blyleven was voted into the **Hall of Fame**.

ABOVE: Rod Carew

KENT HRBEK   First Baseman

• BORN: 5/21/1960   • PLAYED FOR TEAM: 1981 TO 1994

Kent Hrbek was an enormous power hitter who scared opposing pitchers with his home run swing. He was quick and sure-handed in the field, making him one of the Twins' best all-around players.

GARY GAETTI   Third Baseman

• BORN: 8/19/1958   • PLAYED FOR TEAM: 1981 TO 1990

Gary Gaetti was a powerful hitter and a **Gold Glove** fielder, but his biggest contribution was his leadership. With Gaetti on the team, the Twins always felt they had a chance.

KIRBY PUCKETT   Outfielder

• BORN: 3/14/1960   • DIED: 3/6/2006   • PLAYED FOR TEAM: 1984 TO 1995

Kirby Puckett was the most beloved player in Twins history. He led the AL in hits four times, won a batting title, and was a World Series hero twice. Puckett began his career as a singles hitter, but over the years he learned how to use his powerful body to hit home runs.

RICK AGUILERA   Pitcher

• BORN: 12/31/1961   • PLAYED FOR TEAM: 1989 TO 1999

Rick Aguilera was the pitcher the Twins relied on to seal their victories in close games. He had more than 40 **saves** twice for Minnesota and was an All-Star three years in a row.

JOHAN SANTANA   Pitcher

- BORN: 3/13/1979
- PLAYED FOR TEAM: 2000 TO 2007

Johan Santana was discovered by the Twins while pitching in the minor leagues for another team. After adding a **change-up** to his blazing fastball, he became one of the best left-handers in the league. Santana won the **Cy Young Award** in 2004 and 2006.

JUSTIN MORNEAU   First Baseman

- BORN: 5/15/1981
- FIRST YEAR WITH TEAM: 2003

Justin Morneau grew up in Canada, where hockey is king. But baseball was his first love. In just his fourth season with the Twins, Morneau batted .321 with 130 **runs batted in (RBIs)** and was named AL MVP.

JOE MAUER   Catcher

- BORN: 4/19/1983   • FIRST YEAR WITH TEAM: 2004

Joe Mauer was the first player taken in the 2001 **draft**. Five years later, he became the first catcher to lead all of baseball in batting average. Mauer won two more batting crowns, in 2008 and 2009. No catcher had ever done that before.

ABOVE: Johan Santana shows the fans his Cy Young Award.

CALLING THE SHOTS

When the Twins search for a new manager, they don't usually have to look very far. Minnesota likes to hire former players and coaches for the team—people who understand how the Twins play the game. The Washington Senators believed in this idea, too. Bucky Harris managed the Senators three different times from the 1920s to the 1950s. In 1924, Harris was named player-manager of the team at the age of 27. He led the Senators to the pennant in 1924 and 1925.

The owner of those teams was Clark Griffith. He also managed the club for a while. Other players who guided the Senators under Griffith included Walter Johnson, Ossie Bluege, Joe Kuhel, and Joe Cronin. Cronin led the team to the pennant as its player-manager in 1933.

The Twins have also had great success promoting coaches to the manager's position. That is how Billy Martin, Tom Kelly, and Ron Gardenhire got the job. Each led the team to the **playoffs**. Martin

LEFT: Bucky Harris
RIGHT: Ron Gardenhire

had played a few games for the Twins at the end of his career. They kept him as a scout and later as a coach and minor-league manager. In 1969, he became manager of the Twins and led them to first place in the **AL West**.

Kelly had played briefly for the Twins in the 1970s. He became a coach for the team in the 1980s. In 1986, he was hired to run the club. Minnesota fans recognized him from his time as a coach but knew little else about him. They learned what a good teacher he was to the young players. *Veterans* liked him because he kept them focused and relaxed. In 1987, the Twins won the World Series. In 1991, Kelly led the Twins to a second championship.

Rod Gardenhire was the third base coach for Kelly starting in 1990. In 2002, when Kelly retired, Gardenhire became the manager. Unlike the calm, quiet Kelly, "Gardy" was loud and emotional. The Twins played just as well under their new leader. They finished first in the AL Central six times in his first nine years.

ONE GREAT DAY

No one knew what to expect when the 1991 World Series began. The Twins and Atlanta Braves had both finished last in 1990, and now—against all odds—they were playing for the championship. The Twins won the first two games, and then the Braves won the next three. Minnesota fans were confident their team could come back. After all, the Twins had been in the same position in the 1987 World Series, and they captured the championship.

The players were confident, too. Before Game 6, Kirby Puckett made an announcement in the Minnesota locker room. "Jump on board, boys," he said. "I'm going to carry us tonight. Just back me up a little and I'll take us to Game 7!"

Puckett was true to his word. He drove in one run and scored another early in the game. Then, with the score tied 2–2, he raced to the fence and made a fantastic leaping catch to rob Ron Gant of an extra-base hit. Moments later, Puckett drove in his team's

Kirby Puckett celebrates his Game 6 home run against the Atlanta Braves.

third run. The Braves were able to tie the game, and it went into extra innings. The Twins failed to score in the 10th inning. Their chances seemed to be running out. It was time for "Puck" to be a hero again.

Puckett led off the 11th inning against pitcher Charlie Leibrandt. He waited for the veteran to make a mistake, and when he saw the pitch he wanted, he drove a long home run into the left field seats to win the game 4–3. The next day, the Twins and Braves went into extra innings again. Minnesota won 1–0 for the championship.

LEGEND HAS IT

WHO WAS BASEBALL'S UNHAPPIEST CATCHER?

LEGEND HAS IT that Rick Ferrell was. Ferrell was a great

player who made it into the Hall of Fame. But in 1945, at the age of 39, he spent a lot of time scrambling around in the dirt. That year the Senators had four starting pitchers who threw a **knuckleball**. Nothing is harder for a catcher than guessing how this pitch will move on its way to home plate. Ferrell didn't have much luck. He was charged with 21 **passed balls** in 83 games.

ABOVE: Rick Ferrell   **RIGHT**: Harmon Killebrew

WAS HARMON KILLEBREW THE WORST BUNTER IN BASEBALL HISTORY?

LEGEND HAS IT that he was. Killebrew batted nearly 10,000 times, yet he never made a **sacrifice bunt**. Of course, being a slugger, he was rarely asked to do so. But no one in history played as long as Killebrew without at least one successful bunt.

HARMON KILLEBREW

WHICH TWINS SLUGGER WAS TALKED OUT OF A FOOTBALL CAREER BY A UNITED STATES PRESIDENT?

LEGEND HAS IT that Tom Brunansky was. Brunansky hit more than 20 homers six years in a row for the Twins during the 1980s. "Bruno" was a high-school football star in California in the 1970s. He planned to play in college and then make it his living, until he met with former President Richard Nixon. Nixon convinced Brunansky to give up football and pick baseball instead.

When the Twins traded for 20-year-old Francisco Liriano in 2003, they knew he had a chance to be something special. At first, Liriano had his ups and downs. He also suffered an arm injury. But after winning 14 games in 2010, Minnesota fans expected big things from him in 2011.

Instead, Liriano began the year by allowing more than a run an inning in his first five games. Manager Ron Gardenhire and pitching coach Rick Anderson pulled Liriano aside. If he didn't improve, they told him, he might be out of a job.

Liriano faced the White Sox in Chicago on May 3. When he walked the first batter of the game, he could feel the tension in the dugout. The next batter hit a hard line drive, but the Twins turned it into a double play. That gave Liriano confidence. He didn't allow another batter to reach first base until the fourth inning. By then, the Twins had a 1–0 lead.

As the game wore on, Liriano stayed in a groove. No one on the White Sox could get a hit. Liriano gave up a walk in the eighth inning,

Francisco Liriano is the picture of confidence on his 2011 trading card.

but that runner was erased by another double play. He stepped on the mound for the bottom of the ninth with a 1–0 lead. With three more outs, he would have a **no-hitter**.

The first batter bounced a weak grounder to shortstop Matt Tolbert. He threw to first base for the first out. Liriano walked the next batter. Was he getting tired? Apparently not, because the third batter hit a pop fly to Tolbert. Now there were two outs.

Chicago's Adam Dunn walked to the plate. He worked the count to three balls and two strikes. On Liriano's next pitch, Dunn lined the ball toward left field. But Tolbert was there again. He squeezed the ball for the final out. An exhausted Liriano hugged his catcher. He had pitched the seventh no-hitter in team history. "I was running out of gas," he admitted. "I just thank my teammates that they made some great plays behind me tonight."

KIRBY PUCKETT
HERB CARNEAL PRESS BOX
WCCO
twinsbaseball.com
DQ BLIZZARD DQ BLIZZARD DQ BLIZZARD
34

TEAM SPIRIT

When the Twins played in the Metrodome, no place in the world seemed noisier. The fans would stand and scream during tense moments of a game. Their voices would fill the air. During the World Series, baseball fans in other cities got to see how much the people of Minnesota love their club. When Twins fans twirled their Homer Hankies, it looked like a snowstorm in the stands.

The team's *thank you* to the fans was a brand-new ballpark that opened in downtown Minneapolis in 2010. For young fans, there are history lessons everywhere they turn. Gates are numbered after the uniform numbers of famous Twins. A giant Gold Glove lists the Minnesota players who have won the award. And the team's old "shaking hands" logo stands high above center field.

LEFT: Team spirit was never greater than in 2006, when fans and friends gathered to honor the memory of Kirby Puckett. **ABOVE**: Fans waved this Homer Hanky during the 2004 season.

TIMELINE

Bob Allison and Harmon Killebrew were "Twin Terrors" in the 1960s.

1924
The Senators win their only World Series.

1961
The team moves to Minnesota and becomes the Twins.

1965
The Twins win the AL pennant.

1901
The Washington Senators are one of eight teams in the new American League.

1964
Tony Oliva wins the batting championship.

Walter Johnson was the team's first great star.

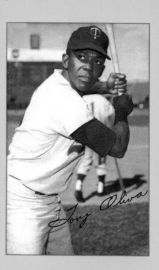

Tony Oliva

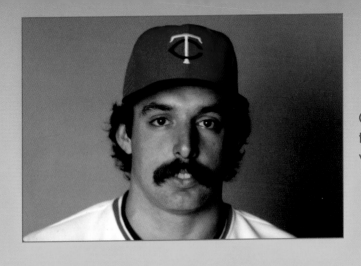

Gary Gaetti led the 1987 Twins with 109 RBIs.

1987
The Twins win their first World Series.

2004
Johan Santana wins the Cy Young Award.

2006
Justin Morneau is named MVP.

1978
Rod Carew wins his seventh batting championship.

1991
The Twins win their second World Series.

2010
Joe Mauer is named MVP.

Johan Santana

Joe Mauer

FUN FACTS

GLOVE STORY

It usually takes great defense to win a pennant, but not always. In 1965, the Twins were AL champs even though they made 172 errors—the most in the league.

OVERSEAS SENSATION

In 2011, the Twins signed Japanese star Tsuyoshi Nishioka to be their second baseman. Nishioka won the 2010 batting title in Japan with a .346 average.

ICE TIME

When Justin Morneau joined the Twins, he picked uniform number 33. Morneau is Canadian, and his favorite athlete as a child was hockey goalie Patrick Roy, who wore that same number.

DOING IT ALL

During the 1960s, Cesar Tovar was the Twins' "do-it-all" player. On September 22, 1968, he really did do it all—he played all nine positions in the same game! When Tovar took the pitcher's mound, one of the batters he faced was slugger Reggie Jackson. Incredibly, he struck Jackson out.

INSIDE BASEBALL

Game 1 of the 1987 World Series—played in the Metrodome—was the first World Series game ever held indoors.

LONG LASTING

Of all the members on the 1961 Twins, pitcher Jim Kaat played the longest, 24 years. He was also one of the only people ever to pitch in four different decades. Kaat started with the Senators in 1959 and finished with the St. Louis Cardinals in 1983.

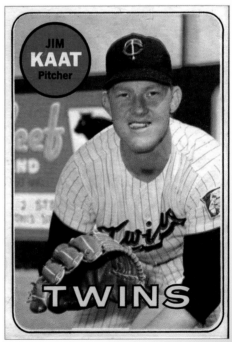

LEFT: Justin Morneau   **RIGHT**: Jim Kaat

TALKING BASEBALL

"I can never thank him enough for all I learned from him. He was a Hall of Famer in every sense of the word."

▶ *ROD CAREW, ON HARMON KILLEBREW*

"I found out early in life that I could hit a baseball farther than most players, and that's what I tried to do."

▶ *HARMON KILLEBREW, ON HIS APPROACH AT THE PLATE*

"He made my life a joy."

▶ *TOM KELLY, ON KIRBY PUCKETT*

"I love Minnesota, and I'd love to play my whole career here."

▶ *JUSTIN MORNEAU, ON WEARING A TWINS UNIFORM*

ABOVE: Harmon Killebrew   **RIGHT**: Torii Hunter

"I'd rather save a home run than hit one."

▶ **TORII HUNTER**, *ON THE THRILL OF MAKING A GREAT CATCH*

"I never let the other team ***dictate*** how I pitched."

▶ **JIM KAAT**, *ON HOW HE TOOK CONTROL OF A GAME*

"I love catching. I love the demands that are put on me and the responsibilities that I have."

▶ **JOE MAUER**, *ON WHY HE CHOSE TO BE A CATCHER*

GREAT DEBATES

People who root for the Twins—and remember the Senators—love to compare their favorite moments, teams, and players. Some debates have been going on for years! How would you settle these classic baseball arguments?

ZOILO VERSALLES HAD THE BEST SEASON OF ANY SHORTSTOP IN TEAM HISTORY ...

… because without him, the Twins would never have won the pennant in 1965. That season, Versalles (**LEFT**) led the AL in doubles, triples, and runs. He also won a Gold Glove and was named the league MVP. A shortstop couldn't be any better than that.

VERSALLES WISHES HE HAD THE SEASON CECIL TRAVIS DID IN 1941 ...

… because Travis was unstoppable. On a team with no other .300 hitters, Travis batted .359 for the Senators and led the AL with 218 hits. He scored 106 runs and drove in 101. If you need to know the difference between these guys as hitters, look at their strikeouts. Versalles led the league with 122 in 1965. Travis had only 25!

... because it saved Game 6 of the 1991 World Series. Puckett soared high to catch Ron Gant's line drive before it hit the fence. It kept the score tied 2–2 and stopped a big inning by the Atlanta Braves. The Twins won Game 6 in extra innings, and then used that *momentum* to take Game 7.

MAYBE SO. BUT THE GREATEST CATCH IN TEAM HISTORY BELONGS TO SAM RICE ...

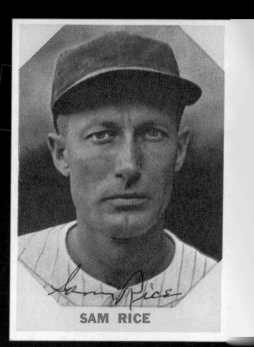

SAM RICE

... because his play in the 1925 World Series was one of baseball's true "unsolved mysteries." With the Senators leading by a run in Game 3 against the Pirates, Rice (RIGHT) leaped into the stands to rob a Pittsburgh hitter of a homer. He then disappeared into a tangle of bodies. It took 15 second for the umpire to make the call. For the rest of Rice's life, friends begged him to tell the truth, "Did you catch it, Sam?" After his death, the Hall of Fame received a note that had been written by Rice. It said, "At no time did I lose possession of the ball."

FOR THE RECORD

T he great Senators and Twins teams and players have left their marks on the record books. These are the "best of the best" …

BOB ALLISON
WASHINGTON SENATORS

Bob Allison

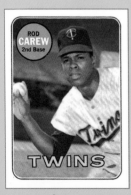

Rod Carew

TWINS AWARD WINNERS

WINNER	AWARD	YEAR
Albie Pearson*	Rookie of the Year**	1958
Bob Allison*	Rookie of the Year	1959
Tony Oliva	Rookie of the Year	1964
Zoilo Versalles	Most Valuable Player	1965
Rod Carew	Rookie of the Year	1967
Harmon Killebrew	Most Valuable Player	1969
Jim Perry	Cy Young Award	1970
Bill Campbell	Reliever of the Year	1976
Rod Carew	Most Valuable Player	1977
John Castino	co-Rookie of the Year	1979
Frank Viola	World Series MVP	1987
Frank Viola	Cy Young Award	1988
Chuck Knoblauch	Rookie of the Year	1991
Tom Kelly	Manager of the Year	1991
Jack Morris	World Series MVP	1991
Marty Cordova	Rookie of the Year	1995
Johan Santana	Cy Young Award	2004
Johan Santana	Cy Young Award	2006
Justin Morneau	Most Valuable Player	2006
Joe Mauer	Most Valuable Player	2010

* Member of the Washington Senators
**The annual award given to each league's best first-year player.

ACHIEVEMENT	YEAR
AL Pennant Winners*	1924
World Series Champions*	1924
AL Pennant Winners*	1925
AL Pennant Winners*	1933
AL Pennant Winners	1965
AL West Champions	1969
AL West Champions	1970
AL West Champions	1987
AL Pennant Winners	1987
World Series Champions	1987
AL West Champions	1991
AL Pennant Winners	1991
World Series Champions	1991
AL Central Champions	2002
AL Central Champions	2003
AL Central Champions	2004
AL Central Champions	2006
AL Central Champions	2009
AL Central Champions	2010

The team played as the Washington Senators.

TWINS
jim perry • pitcher

BERT
BLYLEVEN
MINNESOTA TWINS
PITCHER

TOP: Jim Perry won the 1970 Cy Young Award.
ABOVE: Bert Blyleven won 15 games in 1987.
LEFT: Torii Hunter was an All-Star in 2002.

PINPOINTS

The history of a baseball team is made up of many smaller stories. These stories take place all over the map—not just in the city a team calls "home." Match the pushpins on these maps to the **TEAM FACTS**, and you will begin to see the story of the Twins unfold!

TEAM FACTS

1   Minneapolis, Minnesota—*The Twins have played here since 1982. They played in nearby Bloomington from 1961 to 1981.*

2   Chicago, Illinois—*Kirby Puckett was born here.*

3   St. Louis, Missouri—*The Twins played in the 1987 World Series here.*

4   Hempstead, New York—*Frank Viola was born here.*

5   Washington, D.C.—*The team played here as the Senators from 1901 to 1960.*

6   Atlanta, Georgia—*The Twins played in the 1991 World Series here.*

7   Houston, Texas—*Chuck Knoblauch was born here.*

8   Payette, Idaho—*Harmon Killebrew was born here.*

9   Pinar del Rio, Cuba—*Tony Oliva was born here.*

10   Gatun, Panama Canal Zone—*Rod Carew was born here.*

11   Tovar Merida, Venezuela—*Johan Santana was born here.*

12   Zeist, Netherlands—*Bert Blyleven was born here.*

Kirby Puckett

GLOSSARY

🧠 **AL CENTRAL**—A group of American League teams that play in the central part of the country.

🧠 **AL WEST**—A group of American League teams that play in the western part of the country.

🧠 **ALL-STAR**—A player who is selected to play in baseball's annual All-Star Game.

🧠 **AMERICAN LEAGUE (AL)**—One of baseball's two major leagues; the AL began play in 1901.

⚙️ *ARTIFICIAL*—Made by people, not nature.

🧠 **CHANGE-UP**—A slow pitch disguised to look like a fastball.

🧠 **CY YOUNG AWARD**—The award given each year to each league's best pitcher.

⚙️ *DECADES*—Periods of 10 years; also specific periods, such as the 1950s.

⚙️ *DICTATE*—Control or affect the way something is done.

🧠 **DRAFT**—The annual meeting at which teams take turns choosing the best players in high school and college.

🧠 **GOLD GLOVE**—The award given each year to baseball's best fielders.

🧠 **GRAND SLAM**—A home run with the bases loaded.

🧠 **HALL OF FAME**—The museum in Cooperstown, New York, where baseball's greatest players are honored.

🧠 **KNUCKLEBALL**—A pitch thrown with no spin, which "wobbles" as it nears home plate.

⚙️ *LOGO*—A symbol or design that represents a company or team.

🧠 **MAJOR LEAGUE BASEBALL**—The top level of professional baseball. The American League and National League make up today's major leagues.

🧠 **MINOR LEAGUES**—The many professional leagues that help develop players for the major leagues.

⚙️ *MOMENTUM*—Strength or force built up after a victory.

🧠 **MOST VALUABLE PLAYER (MVP)**—The award given each year to each league's top player; an MVP is also selected for the World Series and the All-Star Game.

🧠 **NO-HITTER**—A game in which a team does not get a hit.

🧠 **PASSED BALLS**—Pitches that get away from the catcher and allow a runner to advance a base.

🧠 **PENNANT**—A league championship. The term comes from the triangular flag awarded to each season's champion, beginning in the 1870s.

⚙️ *PINSTRIPES*—Thin stripes.

🧠 **PLAYER-MANAGER**—A player who also manages his team.

🧠 **PLAYOFFS**—The games played after the regular season to determine which teams will advance to the World Series.

🧠 **RUNS BATTED IN (RBIs)**—A statistic that counts the number of runners a batter drives home.

🧠 **SACRIFICE BUNT**—A bunt intended to advance a runner to his next base.

🧠 **SAVES**—A statistic that counts the number of times a relief pitcher finishes off a close victory for his team.

⚙️ *TRADITION*—A belief or custom that is handed down from generation to generation.

⚙️ *VETERANS*—Players with great experience.

🧠 **WORLD SERIES**—The world championship series played between the American League and National League pennant winners.

EXTRA INNINGS

TEAM SPIRIT introduces a great way to stay up to date with your team! Visit our **EXTRA INNINGS** link and get connected to the latest and greatest updates. **EXTRA INNINGS** serves as a young reader's ticket to an exclusive web page—with more stories, fun facts, team records, and photos of the Twins. Content is updated during and after each season. The **EXTRA INNINGS** feature also enables readers to send comments and letters to the author! Log onto:

www.norwoodhousepress.com/library.aspx

and click on the tab: **TEAM SPIRIT** to access **EXTRA INNINGS**.

Read all the books in the series to learn more about professional sports. For a complete listing of the baseball, basketball, football, and hockey teams in the **TEAM SPIRIT** series, visit our website at:

www.norwoodhousepress.com/library.aspx

ON THE ROAD

MINNESOTA TWINS
1 Twins Way
Minneapolis, Minnesota 55415
(612) 659-3400
minnesota.twins.mlb.com

NATIONAL BASEBALL
HALL OF FAME AND MUSEUM
25 Main Street
Cooperstown, New York 13326
(888) 425-5633
www.baseballhalloffame.org

ON THE BOOKSHELF

To learn more about the sport of baseball, look for these books at your library or bookstore:

• Augustyn, Adam (editor). *The Britannica Guide to Baseball*. New York, NY: Rosen Publishing, 2011.

• Dreier, David. *Baseball: How It Works*. North Mankato, MN: Capstone Press, 2010.

• Stewart, Mark. *Ultimate 10: Baseball*. New York, NY: Gareth Stevens Publishing, 2009.

INDEX

ABOUT THE AUTHOR

MARK STEWART has written more than 50 books on baseball and over 150 sports books for kids. He grew up in New York City during the 1960s rooting for the Yankees and Mets, and was lucky enough to meet players from both teams. Mark comes from a family of writers. His grandfather was Sunday Editor of *The New York Times,* and his mother was Articles Editor of *Ladies' Home Journal* and *McCall's.* Mark has profiled hundreds of athletes over the past 25 years. He has also written several books about his native New York and New Jersey, his home today. Mark is a graduate of Duke University, with a degree in history. He lives and works in a home overlooking Sandy Hook, New Jersey. You can contact Mark through the Norwood House Press website.

ML   3/12